From Faith To FEBA

The Prostitute, the Widow, and the Woman at the Well

Author
Tim Houston
Commentary by
Cantrice Houston

Houston Publishing

ATLANTA, GEORGIA

Tim Houston/Houston Publishing
Loganville, Georgia/30052

Publisher's Note: This is a work of fiction. Names, characters, places, and incidents are a product of the author's imagination. Locales and public names are sometimes used for atmospheric purposes. Any resemblance to actual people, living or dead, or to businesses, companies, events, institutions, or locales is completely coincidental.

Scriptures marked NIV are taken from the NEW INTERNATIONAL VERSION (NIV):Scripture taken from THE HOLY BIBLE, NEW INTERNATIONAL VERSION ®. Copyright©1973, 1978, 1984, 2011 by Biblica, Inc.™. Used by permission of Zondervan

Scriptures marked CEV are taken from the CONTEMPORARY ENGLISH VERSION (CEV): Scripture taken from the CONTEMPORARY ENGLISH VERSION copyright© 1995 by the American Bible Society. Used by permission.

Scriptures marked NLT are taken from the HOLY BIBLE, NEW LIVING TRANSLATION (NLT): Scriptures taken from the HOLY BIBLE, NEW LIVING TRANSLATION, Copyright©1996, 2004, 2007 by Tyndale House Foundation. Used by permission of Tyndale House Publishers, Inc., Carol Stream, Illinois 60188. All rights reserved. Used by permission.

Scriptures marked ISV are taken from the INTERNATIONAL STANDARD VERSION (ISV): Scripture taken from INTERNATIONAL STANDARD VERSION, copyright© 1996-2008 by the ISV Foundation. All rights reserved internationally.

Scriptures marked KJV are taken from the KING JAMES VERSION (KJV): KING JAMESVERSION, public domain.

Scriptures marked ESV are taken from THE HOLY BIBLE, ENGLISH STANDARDVERSION (ESV): Scriptures taken from THE HOLY BIBLE, ENGLISH STANDARD VERSION ® Copyright© 2001 by Crossway, a publishing ministry of Good News Publishers. Used by permission.

Book Layout © 2017 BookDesignTemplates.com

From Faith to FEBA/ Tim Houston. -- 1st ed.
ISBN 978-0-9716746-3-9

To the brave and the courageous who will dare to step out on faith.

Many women do noble things, but you surpass them all.

—PROVERBS 31:29 (NIV)

CONTENTS

Introduction

Women have always played a crucial role in God's plan. From the dawn of time when Eve was introduced as the mother of all living, women have significantly impacted the world. Moses's wife saved him from God's wrath, Sarah's beauty paved the way for Abraham's blessings, Esther's bravery spared her people from destruction, and Mary's devotion to God brought forth the savior of the entire world. For us to positively influence the world, women must. be integral partners in this endeavor. This book, "From Faith to FEBA: The Prostitute, the Widow, and the Woman at the Well; God's Transformational Power in the Lives of Women," celebrates inclusion. It highlights the lives of three women whose stories of triumph amidst tragedy will inspire both women and men.

As I wrote this book, one question I anticipated needing to address is: what does "From Faith to FEBA" mean? Faith is acting on beliefs without visible proof, hence the phrase "we walk by faith and not by sight" (2 Corinthians 5:7). FEBA is a military term meaning "the Forward Edge of the Battle Area," describing the front-most friendly territory on the battlefield and representing a point of no return. In the book, I use **FEBA (Faith, Endurance, Blessings, and Abundance)** to signify a decisive moment where, once committed, the only path is forward. Moving past the FEBA point demands immense faith and courage, fundamentally altering one's life.

Everyone will encounter at least one true "Faith to FEBA " moment in their life. One of my earliest FEBA moments was choosing to join the Marines. Despite having two college scholarship offers as a high-school senior, my circumstances were extraordinary. Two months before graduation, I became a father and needed to provide for my child. Thus, I opted to join the Marines. This decision was not easy, as I knew signing up would irrevocably change my life. Yet, facing my FEBA moment, I took a leap of faith and enlisted. This

1

decision turned out to be one of the best choices I made. Throughout my 13-year Marine Corps career, I supported my family, graduated from college, and traveled the world.

Cantrice's FEBA Moment

My foundational understanding of **F**aith, **E**ndurance, **B**lessings, and **A**bundance originates from my childhood experience of growing up in Chicago Illinois, without an earthly father—a deeply challenging reality. At the age of four, I vividly recall sitting on a barstool, gazing at a photograph while my mother cried out and at that moment, I did not comprehend that I along with my three brothers, had become fatherless children.

The loss I experienced as a little girl prompted me to seek comfort through prayer, initiating my spiritual journey with private conversations with my Heavenly Father. Later, the passing of my brothers, sons, and nephew brought significant challenges. However, these hardships encouraged me to find solace in God while continuously moving forward.

Throughout my life, those experiences have instilled in me the belief that I am not fatherless; my Heavenly Father has been present during both my trials and triumphs. Despite past trauma and mistakes, I have always found refuge and comfort in prayer and worship.

My **FEBA** moment (point of no return) began when faith empowered me to navigate a challenging journey from Chicago to Minnesota, driving a Ford Taurus with two young children while pregnant. In that moment, I felt as though I was leaving behind my spiritual MOAB. My faith in God has been the saving grace in my life. Through prayer and repentance, I have consistently experienced God's mercy and grace.

At present, I observe God's steadfast protection extending to my children, grandchildren, husband, family, and blended family. I am in a period of clarity and look forward with anticipation to what God will accomplish next. My passion lies in offering small, unique, and meaningful gifts that promote self-love and self-care to individuals, letting them know that they are cherished. I believe that a simple smile can make a world of difference.

Where will your Faith to FEBA moment lead you? This book will help you recognize and maximize that moment! The three women featured used faith to move from their life's lows to unimaginable heights. They chose faith over fear. These women were far from ordinary: one was known as a prostitute, another a widow, and the third an outcast. Although unique, they shared a common thread—choosing to leave familiarity behind to reach a destiny attainable only by faith. Their courage to walk by faith allowed them to witness God's transformative power.

Be encouraged! Your "Faith to FEBA" moment is approaching. Read this book attentively, pausing to reflect on parallels with your life's circumstances. Reference the accompanying scriptures against the Bible. Through this, you will discern your FEBA moment and find clarity in your life's direction. Stay steadfast, as the rest of your journey will be driven by conviction, achieving true transformation through faith in God. Maintain an open mind and stay inquisitive.

First, avoid passing judgment or making assumptions. Yes, Rahab was believed to be a prostitute, but her story transcends her assumed profession. She supported her parents, siblings, nieces, and nephews. Today, single mothers face similar challenges providing for their families. Rahab's story showcases the power of her FEBA moment and its positive impact on her family's lives.

Secondly, do not let comfort constrain your vision of future possibilities. Consider Ruth: a widow who had nothing, but through her faithfulness, became everything to Boaz, who needed nothing. Her FEBA moment came when she left the familiar for a place of promise and hope. By embracing possibilities, Ruth found Boaz and inspired countless women.

Thirdly, seize the moment and focus on what's ahead. The woman at the well's "Faith to FEBA" moment resonates with those unable to self-correct their life situations. Encountering Jesus, she seized the moment, invited Him into her life, and allowed transformation. Her

"Faith to FEBA" turned her from an outcast into an evangelist, sharing her experience with the entire city.

Finally, "Faith to FEBA" is about transformation—not mere incremental changes from human actions, but profound conversion through faith in God. This book is for anyone bold enough to leave their comfort zone and embark on a journey of faith. This decision will transform you and those around you for the better. Enjoy the journey of "From Faith to FEBA (Faith, Endurance, Blessings, and Abundance)," witnessing God's transformative power in women's lives!

Rahab: A Journey of Faith and Transformation

Rahab was often identified as "Rahab the prostitute," but that label doesn't capture the essence of who she truly was. Rahab stands out as a formidable biblical figure whose narrative resonates across the spectrum of inclusiveness. Despite being an outsider, she aspired towards belonging. She experienced men at their worst yet placed her trust in two strangers. Born into a non-believing family, her faith was strong enough to save them all. Rahab's identity transcended the labels attached to her, much like how people today are more complex than their public personas. To truly understand someone, one must delve into their story. Greater knowledge of a person's journey fosters deeper understanding and meaningful relationships.

Rahab's tale is unique, especially considering the predominantly male, Hebrew-centric heroes of the Old Testament. While commonly identified as a harlot, deeper exploration reveals more nuances. Rabbinic texts describe her profession with the term "ishah," translating to prostitute, whereas the Aramaic Targum interprets this as innkeeper. During that era, a woman with frequent male visitors would be presumed a harlot. However, this did not hinder Rahab from becoming a woman of faith. When faced with her critical moment, she chose faith over fear. Here's her remarkable story:

Firstly, Rahab resided in Jericho, also referred to as the Promised Land. The New Testament regards her as a woman of faith who assisted the Israelites in capturing Jericho by hiding their spies. This act of bravery compelled Joshua, Israel's leader, to spare her life and that of her family. Rahab's name is honored in the New Testament among the "heroes of faith" for her righteous deeds (Hebrews 11). Beyond these accolades, exploring her story reveals even more fascinating aspects of Rahab.

Secondly, Rahab was exceptional, distinct from other women of her time. She was both a homeowner and the head of her household; her family—including parents, siblings, nieces, and nephews—lived under her roof, authority, and protection. Astonishingly, her father also lived with her, unheard of in those times for a woman to lead a household that included men. Rahab's story mirrors contemporary truths: strong women lead and support their families, irrespective of a man's presence.

Not merely an ordinary homeowner, Rahab's residence was expansive and situated adjacent to Jericho's wall, accommodating her extensive family. The roof of her house was level with the city wall, providing her with a strategic view of external events. This vantage point allowed Rahab invaluable insight during perilous times. Aware of imminent war rumors and the divine promise of their land to the Israelites, Rahab understood the risk her home and family faced should those prophecies come true.

Thirdly, Rahab was not only a businesswoman but also a trusted advisor and a woman of deep faith. Her story, upon further exploration, reveals her vision, foresight, and understanding. Initially, these traits were overshadowed by perceptions of her profession. Yet, navigating a man's world, Rahab maintained discretion and skillfully handled others' secrets. Her reputation was well-established across Canaan, with even Jericho's king knowing of her.

The Power and Challenges of Rahab's Beauty

Rahab was a strikingly beautiful woman, previously cited among the three most attractive women of her time. Her beauty worked to her advantage and made her highly regarded by men. Much like height, intelligence, strength, and wealth, beauty can be considered an asset. Take King Saul for instance; he was chosen as king due to his notable height. Similarly, an attractive woman's appearance can evoke strong desire in men, which they might see as beneficial since they are often willing to provide what is necessary to attain what they want.

In Mark chapter six, King Herod demonstrated this when he offered a young woman up to half of his kingdom, reflecting his immense desire. "When the daughter of Herodias came in and danced, she pleased Herod and his guests. The king said to the girl, 'Ask me for anything you want, and I will give it to you.' And he vowed to her, 'Whatever you ask I will give you, up to half my kingdom!'" (Mark 6:22-23 NIV).

This was the situation for Rahab. Her beauty brought her many blessings, but she soon realized that attractiveness also comes with its own challenges. Attractive women often face stereotypes, such as being labeled gold-diggers or homewreckers. Some men may question their motives, wondering, "If she can be with anyone, why choose me?" To address these doubts, they may compare their assets to those of other men. If they find themselves adequate, they will pursue her earnestly. However, if they feel lacking and possess the means, they might resort to purchasing her time and affection.

For Rahab, these superficial relationships created a yearning for deeper and more meaningful connections. She desired the chance to abandon that lifestyle. As the men visited, she listened attentively to their tales and entertained their promises courteously. Despite this, there was some benefit in these interactions. These cordial exchanges mostly enhanced the value of the gifts she received, and Rahab took pleasure in hearing stories of adventures from across the globe.

Rahab's Transformation: From Transactions to Transcendence

Rahab lived vicariously through the experiences of others. Confined within the walls of Jericho, she cherished tales of adventures in distant lands. Every day, men from faraway places would come to her door, ensuring a constant stream of storytellers. Many would boast about their travels and exploits; Rahab listened carefully as their words served as her books and their journeys as her atlas.

She was particularly captivated by the stories of the children of Israel, which deeply resonated with her. She knew of their initial freedom in Egypt, their subsequent enslavement, and how they called upon God, who sent Moses as their deliverer. Despite being raised in Pharaoh's household, Moses chose to endure hardship with his people, leaving behind the comforts of Egypt and encountering God in the desert. Rahab admired that despite their struggles, the Israelites remained steadfast in their faith.

Rahab paid attention to the nuances of these stories, including Moses' marriage to Zipporah, a Midianite. As a Canaanite herself, Rahab found hope in this narrative, envisioning a new life elsewhere. She drew inspiration from how Moses included his father-in-law, Jethro (Reuel), and his brother-in-law, Hobab, in the journey out of Egypt. Reuel became an advisor to Moses, and Hobab was described as their "eyes" in the wilderness. These accounts allowed Rahab to imagine her family being similarly welcomed.

Although the precise moment of Rahab's belief in God is unknown, the author of Hebrews asserts her faith. This belief marked the beginning of her FEBA (Faith, Endurance, Blessings, and Abundance) journey. Rahab's faith required action, which would propel her to a decisive point where there was no turning back.

Rahab understood that the Lord had granted the Israelites victory over their enemies, despite them being former slaves with no military expertise, organized army, or king. Their successful conquests of the Amorite kings Sihon and Og caused fear throughout Jericho, demoralizing its people and unsettling its king. The king's confidence lay in the belief that Jericho's walls were impregnable, and he ordered the gates shut at sunset for additional security. Yet, Rahab perceived differently.

Her newfound faith was soon put to test when two Israelites spies arrived at her home. Understanding the city's lack of secrets, Rahab quickly and quietly invited them in. She hid them on her roof amongst stalks of flax and devised a story to mislead the king's soldiers who would inevitably follow. This act of hiding the spies without securing an agreement exposed her to significant risk—a true point of no return.

As anticipated, word reached Jericho's king about the spies at Rahab's place. He dispatched soldiers to investigate, but Rahab was ready. Confident the spies were well hidden under the flax, she met the soldiers at her door and relayed her premeditated story. She claimed the spies left before the gates closed and urged the soldiers to pursue them quickly. Convinced by her tale, the soldiers hastily departed the city without searching her house. Now that the soldiers had left, Rahab returned to the roof to present her request.

"I KNOW THE LORD HAS GIVEN YOU THIS LAND," SHE TOLD THEM. "WE ARE ALL AFRAID OF YOU. EVERYONE IN THE LAND IS LIVING IN TERROR, FOR WE HAD HEARD HOW THE LORD MADE A DRY PATH FOR YOU THROUGH THE RED SEA WHEN YOU LEFT EGYPT. AND WE KNOW WHAT YOU DID TO SIHON AND OG, THE TWO AMORITE KINGS EAST OF THE JORDAN RIVER, WHOSE PEOPLE YOU COMPLETELY DESTROYED. NO WONDER OUR HEARTS HAVE MELTED IN FEAR! NO ONE HAS THE COURAGE TO FIGHT AFTER HEARING SUCH THINGS. FOR THE LORD, YOUR GOD IS THE SUPREME GOD OF THE HEAVENS ABOVE AND THE EARTH BELOW. "NOW SWEAR TO ME BY THE LORD THAT YOU WILL BE KIND TO ME AND MY FAMILY SINCE I HAVE HELPED YOU. GIVE ME

SOME GUARANTEE THAT WHEN JERICHO IS CONQUERED,
YOU WILL LET ME LIVE, ALONG WITH MY FATHER AND
MOTHER, MY BROTHERS AND SISTERS, AND ALL THEIR
FAMILIES." (JOSHUA 2:8-13 NLT)

The men of Israel listened to Rahab's request and entered into a covenant with her that day, with three conditions. First, she had to vow to keep their secret. Second, she and her entire family had to remain inside her house, as they would be killed if found outside when Israel captured the city. Third, she needed to hang a scarlet rope from her window so the Israelites could identify her house. Rahab agreed to these terms and used a scarlet rope to lower the men out the window. The men then hid in the mountains for three days until the search ended and subsequently returned to Joshua's camp to report their findings.

After they left, Rahab tied the scarlet rope to her window, marking her acceptance of the covenant. As she secured it, she might have remembered the story of the Israelites' exodus from Egypt, where they marked their doorposts with blood to ensure protection from the final plague. This act was part of Moses' covenant with God, and Rahab believed that the same divine promise would protect her. One can imagine her smiling as she tightened the rope on the window.

Rahab now faced significant challenges. Firstly, she had to persuade her family to stay indoors, a difficult task as they were not part of the initial agreement. Nevertheless, out of respect for her, they complied. Secondly, she needed to ration the food without knowing how long it would have to last, since the men did not provide a timeline or return date. Despite her new faith, she had to trust in God through this test. Thirdly, she had to keep the secret about hiding the men, which meant closing her business and resisting public speculation and gossip.

Lastly, Rahab had to maintain her faith amidst uncertainty. She had numerous questions with few answers: How would the Israelites cross the Jordan River? How would they breach Jericho's walls? Would they remember her? What if the spies were killed? Would someone else uphold their agreement? These and other thoughts might have troubled her, yet having passed the point of no return, she and her family had no choice but to wait and believe.

The Waiting of Rahab

For Rahab, the first three days were likely the easiest. She was aware that the two men were in the mountains, waiting for the search party to return. Afterward, the wait became more challenging. Unbeknownst to her, the Israelites had moved from Shittim to the Jordan River, and Joshua, their leader, had decided to stay there for three days. Thus, for Rahab, it became six days with no return. It would then take an additional three days for the entire Israelite camp to cross the Jordan River. Nine days into the covenant agreement between Rahab and the spies, she and her family remained confined indoors. Although they were unaware of the developments within the Israelite camp, Rahab's faith ensured that none of her family ventured outside.

Then a miracle occurred! The Israelites crossed the Jordan on dry land, and the news spread rapidly! When the Amorite and Canaanite kings on the other side of the Jordan heard, fear gripped them, and they lost the will to fight the Israelites. This was great news for Joshua because God had other plans for them. Crossing the Jordan River symbolized a spiritual baptism, marking the Israelites' entry into a new covenant, which would be a blood covenant. God commanded Joshua to circumcise all the men who crossed over with him. The blood of this covenant would remove the stigma of their slavery in Egypt. Joshua obeyed, naming the place Gilgal, signifying a fresh start for the Israelites.

Rahab and her family were fortunate as Joshua was a man of faith. Despite being in enemy territory, he was unafraid to incapacitate his entire army. All the men, including those in the army, underwent circumcision, which took four days. They were unfit to fight and needed a week to recover. Rahab and her family continued to wait, 20 days into the covenant, as the men of Israel recuperated. Although unaware of these events, Rahab and her family stayed indoors, not breaking the covenant.

Joshua, on a mission from God, provided the Israelites with corn from Canaan and manna from heaven, symbolic of the Passover feast as part of their new covenant in the new land. God was with them. As Joshua gazed towards Jericho, he encountered a man with a drawn sword. Upon questioning whether he was an adversary, the man identified himself as a captain of the Lord's host. Joshua worshipped, recognizing it was the Lord. The captain of the Lord's host instructed Joshua to remove his shoes, declaring the ground holy, and Joshua complied.

This encounter validated Joshua's mission. According to Psalms 34:7, "The angel of the Lord encamps around those who fear him, and he delivers them." The Israelites were protected, enclosed by the Lord's angels. In Jericho, Rahab was safe too. Despite the turmoil and fear gripping the city at the arrival of the Israelites, Rahab and her family were secure inside.

Rahab perhaps sensed her deliverance approaching. During this crucial time, she comforted her family, keeping their faith strong. The two men had assured her they would spare her family, and Rahab trusted their words, so despite 20 uncertain days, everyone remained inside.

In the Israelite camp, God enacted His plan. Warriors led the ark of the covenant, marching silently around Jericho's walls for six days. On the seventh day, accompanied by priests and trumpeters, they marched around the walls seven times. Following the seventh circuit, the trumpets blared, the people shouted loudly, and Jericho's walls collapsed! The Israelites adhered to Joshua's instructions, and on the seventh day, after their marching and shouts, the walls came tumbling down!

Twenty-seven days into the wait, Rahab needed no announcement: her house stood by the walls. The collapse shook her home's foundation! Though the thunderous fall could have incited fear, Rahab and her household stayed indoors, maintaining their belief in God. The Israelites entered the city, sparing no one. The violence reached Rahab's door. Faced with calamity, would Rahab run in fear or hold onto her faith? Rahab chose to trust in God.

Joshua sent men to her home, where the two spies she had helped appeared. They honored their promise! Escorting Rahab and her family into Israel's camp, they upheld their word. The Bible sums up these events best!

"AND JOSHUA SAVED RAHAB THE PROSTITUTE, HER FAMILY, AND ALL THOSE WHO WERE WITH HER. JOSHUA LET THEM LIVE BECAUSE RAHAB HELPED THE SPIES JOSHUA HAD SENT OUT TO JERICHO. RAHAB STILL LIVES AMONG THE ISRAELITES TODAY" (JOSHUA 6:25 ERV).

Joshua saved Rahab, and while the world still referred to her as "Rahab the harlot," God transformed her internally. Despite her house being destroyed along with the rest of Jericho, her faith in God ensured the survival of her and her family. Rahab's story endures, as she is commemorated among the heroes of faith.

"BY FAITH RAHAB THE PROSTITUTE DID NOT PERISH WITH THOSE WERE DISOBEDIENT, BECAUSE SHE HAD GIVEN A FRIENDLY WELCOME TO THE SPIES" (HEBREWS 11:31 ESV)

Rahab, once identified as a harlot, transformed into a woman of faith. Such a remarkable change illustrates Jesus' words: "All things are possible for the one who believes" (Mark 9:23). Through faith, one can become entirely renewed.

Rahab's Remarkable Journey

Where Rahab's tale ends in the Book of Joshua, it continues in the Book of Ruth. Although her journey from Jericho is not documented, there is no doubt she faced numerous challenges that made her journey very difficult.

Firstly, Rahab was a foreigner, and the Israelites were taught not to marry outside their race and culture. Additionally, people would remain suspicious of her motives since no one witnessed her conversion. Women in the camp might be jealous and distrustful of her beauty. Furthermore, individuals could resent her because she was favored by God. To manage these challenges, Rahab would need to keep a low profile, although this would be easier said than done.

Unfortunately, Rahab could not hide the fact that she was a foreigner, one of her biggest hurdles since even Israel's top leaders opposed intermarriage. For instance, consider the story of Miriam, Moses's sister, who was struck with leprosy for criticizing Moses's marriage to an Ethiopian woman. They questioned his leadership due to his marriage, but God intervened and punished Miriam with leprosy.

Another significant challenge was proving her conversion. The Israelites only knew her as "Rahab the prostitute," and with Jericho destroyed for its wickedness, she was seen as one of its notorious citizens. Except for Joshua and the two spies, the other Israelites viewed her as an enemy. Rahab had to ignore the whispers and taunting that followed her around, which was undoubtedly painful. She needed to remember that while people's opinions matter, what God says matters most. For Rahab, the inner peace from knowing God had to suffice.

Additionally, Rahab's past posed problems. Men still desired her, and women continued to despise her. To minimize this, she needed to limit interactions with men and be "nice" to the women, relying on her family's company to avoid any hint of impropriety. Despite her efforts, she would be recognized as "Rahab the prostitute" throughout both the Old and New Testament.

Lastly, Rahab would be resented for being favored by God. Among all the families in Jericho, only her family was saved. Joshua not only spared her life but integrated her into the Israelite community. However, Rahab soon realized that God's favor often brings human scorn. Jesus told his disciples, "If the world hates you, keep in mind that they hated me first" (John 15:18).

Even today, people struggle to accept that God favors those outside social norms. Individuals like to determine who is considered "good." When God favors the "not so good," believers are scrutinized. During Jesus's time, people questioned His interactions with tax collectors and sinners and doubted His godliness when a woman washed His feet with her tears. Similarly, they called Him a sinner for healing a blind man on the Sabbath. If Jesus's relationships were challenged, ours will certainly be questioned today.

Rahab's Redemption and Legacy

Rahab enters this phase of her life as a strong, experienced, determined, and independent woman. This transformation was made possible through her relationship with God. When they entered the promised land, she remained the provider for her family, requiring that her partner be confident enough to accept her fully. Despite her notoriety, Rahab couldn't seek out a husband; he would have to find her. Miraculously, through God's grace, he did!

Like Rahab herself, her story of meeting her husband is private, and we must examine it closely to uncover it. Although she is not mentioned by name in the book of Ruth, her story certainly is. Rahab put her trust in God and waited patiently. Despite her difficulties, personal history, and public reputation, she met Salmon. He quietly and privately married her.

Salmon, now Rahab's husband, came from a notable Hebrew lineage. He was an ancestor of both David and Jesus Christ. His father, Nahshon, was Aaron's brother-in-law (Moses' brother) and the leader of the tribe of Judah (Numbers 7:12). Even though the tribe of Judah was fourth among the Patriarchs, Nahshon was noteworthy because during the dedication of the Tabernacle, he was the first to present his dedicatory offering. Both Nahshon and Salmon were forefathers of King David, and their stories are interconnected with Rahab's story.

Who could have imagined that Rahab, by the grace and providence of God, would marry into the Jewish royal lineage? Rahab's conversion illustrates God's transformative power in a woman's life! Rahab exemplifies perseverance. Through her faith journey, she faced significant challenges and courageously moved beyond her turning point. By choosing to trust God, her life was radically changed! What could your life become if you dared to believe in God? Where might your faith lead you?

Rahab's story of courageous faith continues beyond the book of Ruth into the New Testament, and her testimony still resonates today! Rahab chose to trust God, and He blessed her for it. Matthew 1:5-6 states it clearly: "Salmon was the father of Boaz by Rahab, Boaz the father of Obed by Ruth, Obed the father of Jesse, and Jesse the father of David the king." Rahab became the mother of Boaz and the mother-in-law of Ruth. She is listed among the heroes of faith, showcasing God's transformational power in her life!

SALMON WAS THE FATHER OF BOAZ BY RAHAB, BOAZ THE FATHER OF OBED BY RUTH, OBED THE FATHER OF JESSE, AND JESSE THE FATHER OF DAVID THE KING. (MATTHEW 1:5-6)

Cantrice's Commentary:
Part One: Rahab, The Story of Redemption

I was intrigued to read about Rahab's story. She was a prominent figure found in the Bible, especially within the Old Testament book of Joshua. She lived in Jericho, a fortified Canaanite city. As the Israelites, under Joshua's leadership, prepared to take over Jericho, Rahab's story unfolded when she played a pivotal role by assisting the Israelite spies.

Reading about Rahab fascinated me, as she was continually referred to as "Rahab the prostitute" throughout the Bible, including in the New Testament (Hebrews 11:31). Josephus, the Jewish historian of the first century, describes Rahab as an innkeeper. The Hebrew consonant can refer either to a prostitute or a woman who provides food and shelter. It's remarkable that this powerful, extraordinary, nurturing, and caring woman of God is remembered by a label others assigned her.

When I learned that the Hebrew term describing her profession was "ishah", meaning "innkeeper," used in the Targum, it resonated with me. Consider that she lived with her family. Would influential men really expose their sins in such an environment? Unfortunately, observers who saw many men visit her home could only think of the word "harlot."

This mislabeling still happens today. How many women are misjudged based on others' perceptions? Instead of being appreciated for their skills and talents, they're often defined by tarnished labels imposed by others. The Bible never mentions Rahab engaging with men sexually or referring to herself as a prostitute. She was labeled, and this designation followed her into the New Testament.

Yet, Rahab quietly reshaped her narrative. She helped the spies, married Salmon, mothered Boaz, and became King David's great-great-grandmother, one of only five women mentioned in Jesus' lineage! What a journey!

When people don't know your story, they imagine one, usually negative. Successful women might be thought to have slept their way to the top, seen as gold-diggers, or not qualified. These stereotypes force women into defensive positions, hiding their dreams. Even Mary, Jesus's mother, pondered things in her heart without freely sharing them (Luke 2:19 NIV).

Like Mary, Rahab had significant plans but knew she would need men's help to bring them to life eventually. Mary trusted the gospel writer Luke to capture her emotions and passion accurately. Rahab didn't have such an ally; her story was told by men unaware of her heart's love for God and her thoughtful plans. Rahab recognized God's supremacy and entrusted two unknown men because they were his servants. She convinced her family to stay indoors for 27 days, providing for them all.

For today's women, who will tell your story? Is it someone who truly knows you, or are you documenting your own thoughts? If not, start a diary, keep a journal—tell your story! The wonders in your heart are incredible because you are naturally powerful. Every woman is. Created with life and the ability to give life, her experiences are vital to her story.

Regardless of labels others impose, remember the name Jesus gave you surpasses them all! "I will also give that person a white stone with a new name written on it, known only to the one who receives it." Revelation 2:17b NIV. Dare to believe God for the unthinkable! Dare to share your story! The world needs your voice!

Cantrice

Summary of Rahab:
Key Points and Scriptures

Journey of Faith and Transformation

Introduction

As a woman, Rahab's story speaks profoundly to the power of faith and transformation. Seen initially for her profession, Rahab's journey showcases resilience, courage, and unwavering belief in God's promises. Her experience is a testament to how faith can elevate one's circumstances, regardless of past labels or societal judgments.

Key Points

- Faith Over Fear: Rahab's decision to hide the two Israeli spies demonstrated her trust in God's plan over the imminent danger she faced.
- Breaking Societal Norms: In a time when women were rarely heads of households, Rahab not only led her family but also made critical decisions that ensured their survival.
- Resilience and Redemption: Rahab's past did not define her future. Her faith marked a turning point, leading to her integration into the Israelite community and her marriage to Salmon.
- God's Favor: Despite her past, Rahab was favored by God, leading to her inclusion in the lineage of King David and, ultimately, Jesus Christ.

Scriptures

Joshua 2:8-13: "I know the Lord has given you this land... For the Lord your God is the supreme God of the heavens above and the earth below."

Hebrews 11:31: "By faith Rahab the prostitute did not perish with those who were disobedient, because she had given a friendly welcome to the spies."

Matthew 1:5-6: "Salmon was the father of Boaz by Rahab, Boaz the father of Obed by Ruth, Obed the father of Jesse, and Jesse the father of David the king."

Mark 9:23: "All things are possible for the one who believes."

Conclusion

Rahab's story is a powerful reminder that God can use anyone to fulfill His divine purposes, regardless of their past. Her faith exemplifies the transformative power of belief, demonstrating how God's grace can redefine one's life. As women, we should draw inspiration from Rahab's courage and unwavering faith, recognizing that our own "Faith to FEBA (Faith, Endurance, Blessings, and Abundance)" moments can lead to extraordinary transformations.

Ruth: The Unexpected Matriarch

The story of Ruth is a captivating narrative captured in the Bible in an Old Testament book that bears her name. Set during the era of the judges in Israel, it starts with Ruth's unwavering loyalty to her mother-in-law Naomi after their husbands have passed away. Tragically, Naomi lost her husband and sons. This book beautifully recounts the tale of a young woman who, despite her tragic circumstances, bravely left her home in pursuit of a better life. Born in a barren land and unable to bear children even after a decade of marriage, Ruth's journey highlights her deep bond with Naomi, a relationship through which she eventually meets her future husband. Her life underscores the theme of God's redeeming power.

In the Gospel of Matthew, Ruth is listed among the ancestors of King David and Jesus, marking her significant as one of only five women named in Jesus' genealogy (the others being Mary, Tamar, Rahab, and Bathsheba). Although widely accepted from biblical accounts, there remains more to explore about Ruth's story. Questions arise about her background, cultural customs, and family dynamics that led her to leave her homeland. What made her closer to Naomi than her own family? What was her connection to Rahab, and why was it important?

Firstly, Ruth hailed from Moab, a nation infamously founded through incest by Lot's daughters, who conceived sons—Ammon and Moab—after getting their father drunk. Ruth, through no fault of her own, came from a country with a stigma and was looked down upon by the Israelites, which likely affected her self-esteem and sense of worth. Similar to Ruth, many women today face issues of self-worth due to circumstances beyond their control.

Secondly, Moab had other negative associations. Geographically near the Promised Land, it was avoided by Israelites in route to Jericho. The Israelites only stopped in Moab because of Moses' death, and the land's reputation as the place where Moses died furthered its negative perception.

Thirdly, Ruth grew up under a different religious system, worshiping the false god Chemosh, which demanded human sacrifices, including children. This practice was detested by the Israelites, who were forbidden by God from accepting Moabites into the temple assembly for ten generations (Deuteronomy 23:3). These factors would have compounded Ruth's low self-esteem.

Eventually, Elimelech from Bethlehem-Judah arrived in Moab with his wife, Naomi, and their two sons, Mahlon and Chilion, seeking food during a famine. After Elimelech's death, Naomi stayed in Moab with her sons, who later married Ruth and Orpah. Ruth wed Mahlon, while Orpah married Chilion.

A Land of Sorrow

Although the details of Ruth and Mahlon's meeting are not documented, it is accepted that they met and married. This union would have been difficult for Ruth, as she married an Israelite—a people who looked down on Moabites and avoided traveling through their land. However, due to a famine in his homeland, Elimelech and his family sought refuge in Moab, essentially seeking help from those they had previously disdained. Ruth's marriage to Mahlon, therefore, likely strained her relationship with both her family and society.

Despite these challenges, Ruth and Mahlon remained married for ten years, but Ruth did not bear any children. The Bible does not provide an explanation as to why this young couple was unable to have children, yet they continued their efforts to conceive. Then tragedy struck suddenly when Mahlon died, shattering Ruth's hopes of motherhood. To compound this sorrow, Naomi's other son, Chilion, also passed away, leaving both Ruth and Orpah widowed and childless.

The deaths of Naomi's sons left her devastated, without husband, sons, or prospects of grandchildren. Overwhelmed by grief, Ruth and Orpah joined Naomi in widowhood. For Naomi, Moab had become a place of immense sorrow, reaffirming its negative reputation she had heard of for years. She decided to return to her homeland in Bethlehem-Judah. Given that Ruth and Orpah had been ostracized by their families for marrying outside their culture, they opted to accompany Naomi on her journey back.

Initially, Naomi, Ruth, and Orpah set out together. However, after traveling a short distance, Naomi paused for a heartfelt conversation with her daughters-in-law. Knowing there would be nothing for them in Judah and having no more sons to offer, Naomi suggested they return to their families. Even if miraculously, she were to bear sons, they would be too old by the time the children came of age. Naomi believed that their only hope lay in returning home, where their families might accept them back, possibly allowing them to remarry and bear children.

With tears, Naomi implored Ruth and Orpah to leave her and return to their homes. They wept together, and both Ruth and Orpah initially refused, declaring, "Surely we will return with you to your people!" Yet Naomi felt it unwise for them to accompany her, as she had no means to support them and feared they would face ostracism for being Moabites. Convinced that God's hand was against her, Naomi did not wish for Ruth and Orpah to suffer alongside her supposed divine punishment.

The Unshakable Devotion of Ruth

Ruth faced a pivotal moment in her life. She had no children and Naomi was heading home, with or without her. This was Ruth's decisive moment, a point of no return. Similarly, Oprah had to make her own decision. The three women—Ruth, Oprah, and Naomi—cried together until they could cry no more. Eventually, Oprah made the sorrowful choice to return to her family, bidding Naomi farewell with a heavy heart. Her departure was profoundly painful for both Naomi and Ruth, as Oprah had been part of their family for many years. As noted in the Bible, Ruth clung to Naomi even more tightly (Ruth 1:14).

Naomi was concerned for Ruth and tried to use Oprah's departure as a reason for Ruth to return home as well. Faced with a critical decision, Ruth had to choose between returning to the familiar Moab with Oprah or following Naomi into the unknown. Ultimately, Ruth concluded that her time in Moab was over; she opted to leave a land of bitterness for one of hope and possibilities. Such a transformation is what happens when faith in God confronts the unimaginable.

Ruth responded to Naomi, pleading, "Please don't urge me to leave you! Wherever you go, I will go; where you live, I will live. Your people will be my people, and your God my God. Where you die, I will die, and there will I be buried. May the Lord deal with me, be it ever so severely, if anything but death separates us!" (Ruth 1:16-17). In this defining moment, Ruth embraced faith over fear, choosing the God of Abraham, Isaac, and Joseph over the gods of the Moabites. Naomi witnessed Ruth's transformation clearly, sensing it in her voice and seeing it in her eyes. From then on, Naomi never asked Ruth to leave again.

The Journey to New Beginnings

Ruth was prepared for her new beginning. The famine had ended, and God's blessings were now upon the land of Judah. Judah, meaning "Praise," had its renowned city Bethlehem, known as "the house of bread and meat." Bethlehem holds a significant place in Israel's history, being where Rachel, Joseph's wife, was buried. With faith, Ruth proclaimed that this would also be her final resting place. She left behind a place associated with desolation and incest to journey towards a land of praise, abundant with milk and honey. Though she had been childless in Moab, Ruth now had faith.

The journey from Moab to Bethlehem-Judah spanned about 50 miles over steep and rugged terrain, taking around 10 days. Ruth was undeterred. Step by step, she and Naomi traveled towards Bethlehem. Entering the city was a joyous moment for Ruth as the long and tiring journey concluded. Inwardly, she felt transformed and full of new faith in God. For Ruth, Moab symbolized death, while Judah represented life and the hope of motherhood. Ruth held onto this hope.

Naomi, however, did not share Ruth's optimism. When word spread throughout Bethlehem about their arrival, the women came out to meet them. They wondered if the older woman was indeed Naomi, whom they hadn't seen for many years. Upon recognizing her, they called out her name, "Naomi," but Naomi's heart remained heavy with grief for the loss of her husband and sons. She asked them to call her Mara, meaning "bitterness," because she believed God had dealt bitterly with her. She lamented that she left Bethlehem full, with a husband and two sons, but returned empty due to their deaths.

Ruth had a different perspective. Her new-found faith in God made her believe that He could bless her with a husband and child despite her being a widow and a foreigner considered second-class by the Israelites. Ruth entrusted herself to God's plan. Meanwhile, she decided to work in the fields for food, unaware that she would be led to a field owned by Boaz, a relative of Naomi's deceased husband Elimelech.

The next day, Ruth went to glean corn that the harvesters missed. Her intention was to find a field to work in early that morning, but God's plan was greater—she was meant to meet Boaz. Boaz was the son of Rahab and Salmon. At this time, Boaz was nearly 80 years old, and both Rahab and Salmon were likely deceased. Although Rahab is not directly mentioned in the Book of Ruth, she and Salmon are noted as Boaz's parents in Jesus' genealogy. While Ruth and Rahab would never meet, they remained connected through Boaz and their shared faith in God.

With godly confidence, Ruth entered Boaz's field. Despite being dressed for labor, her inner and outer beauty shone brightly. Filled with hope, love, and peace from God, Ruth prayed for grace and favor that morning. As she worked, her faith showed in her smile. Ruth would soon discover that Boaz was a man devoted to God.

The Providential Encounter

Ruth did not meet Boaz immediately. She began her work early in the morning. As the new day started, Ruth saw the potential and power of God. As far as she could see, the fields were full of wheat. God's ability to reproduce was evident. For Ruth, even the leftovers would be more than enough to meet her needs. God had given her the strength to work, and she intended to use it to glorify Him.

Unbeknownst to Ruth, Boaz was in Bethlehem when she started working. When he arrived at his field, he demonstrated his faith in God by greeting the reapers with "The Lord be with thee," to which they responded, "The Lord bless thee." Boaz was a man of faith who openly acknowledged God's blessings. His exchange with the harvesters reinforced his belief that God was the one blessing them. After experiencing years of harsh famine, Boaz's faith in God contributed to his ongoing success. God blessed him so that he could, in turn, bless others, and Ruth would benefit from this.

Boaz, a godly employer who knew all his workers by name, did not recognize Ruth when he saw her. He asked his overseer, "Who is that woman?" The overseer, unaware of her name, shared what he had heard about Ruth: she was the Moabite woman who returned from Moab with Naomi. He also noted that Ruth had requested permission to glean in his fields, coming early in the morning and working diligently with few breaks. Impressed, Boaz called for Ruth.

Boaz was immediately attracted to Ruth, as described in Ruth 2:8-9: "Then Boaz said to Ruth, 'My daughter, listen to me. Don't go and glean in another field and don't go away from here. Stay here with the women who work for me. Watch the field where the men are harvesting and follow along after the other women. I have told the men not to lay a hand on you. And whenever you are thirsty, go and get a drink from the water jars the men have filled.'" Ruth was overwhelmed by his generosity and bowed down, asking, "Why have I found such favor in your eyes, and why did you even notice me, since I am a foreigner?" (Ruth 2:10).

Ruth's story and her faith in God would lead to Boaz blessing her. Her tragic circumstances would turn into triumph. Boaz admired her kindness toward Naomi and her courage in leaving her parents to live among strangers. He may have been reminded of his mother Rahab, who also trusted in God and left her homeland. He knew firsthand about the wonderful life his father and mother had despite her difficult past, reflecting some characteristics of his mother in Ruth. Boaz was so captivated by her that he spoke blessings over her life.

"May the LORD repay you for what you have done. May you be richly rewarded by the LORD, the God of Israel, under whose wings you have come to take refuge." (Ruth 2:12 NIV) Ruth was blessed by Boaz because of her kindness to Naomi and her faith in God. Boaz acted as a priest by blessing her, as a provider by ensuring she had food and water, and as a protector by instructing others not to harm her. These roles resemble those of a husband, which Boaz demonstrated upon meeting Ruth.

Thrilled by Boaz's blessing, Ruth called him "lord" and expressed her gratitude for his favor and kind words. Despite being surrounded by many other women, Boaz's actions and words clearly showed his interest in Ruth. Boaz invited Ruth to join him for dinner, which she gladly accepted after a long day without eating. She ate with the servants, careful not to overindulge or behave inappropriately. After finishing her meal, she returned to work, which impressed Boaz. Though watching from afar, he enjoyed her company and was disappointed by her departure.

Ruth continued working diligently, aware that Boaz had made her task easier by ensuring plenty of barley. Following the designated path, she collected over a bushel of barley. Ruth recognized that Boaz's intervention contributed to her success. She presented herself as hardworking, faithful, humble, and appreciative, while Boaz appeared considerate, compassionate, and generous.

Boaz continued to facilitate Ruth's work, allowing her to gather wheat freely and instructing the workers not to correct her. Throughout the day, he deliberately left piles of barley for her to collect, making his intentions clear to everyone. Boaz's genuine interest in Ruth was evident, and his efforts increased Ruth's loyalty to his fields.

A Divine Encounter

It was an exceptional day for Ruth, who returned home brimming with excitement. She promptly shared the barley she had collected with her mother-in-law. Naomi was astounded by the sheer quantity of wheat Ruth had gathered and sensed that someone had blessed her. She affirmed to Ruth that whoever assisted her would also be blessed. Ruth disclosed that while she knew little about the man who had helped her, his name was Boaz. This news greatly thrilled Naomi. "The Lord bless him!" Naomi exclaimed to her daughter-in-law. "He has not stopped showing his kindness to the living and the dead," she continued. "That man is our close relative; he is one of our guardian-redeemers" (Ruth 2:20 NIV). Naomi felt a renewed spirit, confident that God's hand was once again guiding her life.

A guardian-redeemer refers to a person obligated under law to rescue a family member in dire circumstances (Leviticus 25:25-55). The man interested in Ruth happened to be a close relative of Naomi. Aware of this biblical provision, Naomi believed Boaz was equally informed. Naomi expressed open gratitude to the Lord as her bitterness, symbolized by the name Mara she had given herself, was no longer present. Through the guardian-redeemer's provision, Naomi felt blessed. When an individual steps into their purpose and destiny, those around them also benefit.

NAOMI WAS BLESSED BECAUSE RUTH WAS BLESSED!

Although God was with Ruth, she did not find shortcuts to her destiny. Ruth labored from morning until evening throughout the harvest season. She not only worked diligently but also avoided any appearance of trouble. As a result, the only feedback Boaz received about her was that she was a hard worker. Even in her labor, Ruth conducted herself with honor and distinction, which led Boaz to continue rewarding her. Are you actively working toward your blessing, or are you waiting for someone to rescue you from it? Are you striving towards your destiny despite your circumstances? Hard work and dedication are essential for success in God's eyes. These qualities must be demonstrated consistently. Ruth continued to work diligently and faithfully.

Once the harvest season ended, Naomi became concerned. Winter was approaching, and she knew Ruth wouldn't be able to collect barley anymore. To survive through winter, Ruth would need to marry. Time was of the essence as the men would soon return to their homes, and there would be no available suitors for Ruth. Naomi believed Boaz would be a good provider for Ruth and could offer her a permanent home.

Boaz, being a relative and a guardian-redeemer, worked late into the night processing barley seeds. Naomi knew that the place where barley was processed was airy and very cold at night. She instructed Ruth to go to Boaz that night and lie at his feet to warm him. Ruth agreed, but instead of wearing the work clothes Boaz was accustomed to seeing her in, she bathed, perfumed herself, and put on her best clothes. That night, Boaz would see Ruth in all her beauty; even if he couldn't see her clearly in the dark, he would know she was there by the warmth of her presence and the fragrance of her aroma.

When Blessings Converge

Naomi wanted Ruth to make a positive impact on Boaz. She advised Ruth not to reveal her presence until Boaz had finished his meal and drink, to avoid the risk of him sending her away prematurely. Ruth heeded Naomi's advice: she identified the place where Boaz would sleep and remained hidden until he finished eating and drinking. Boaz, in high spirits, laid down and fell asleep. Once he was asleep, Ruth emerged from her hiding spot and gently laid at his feet, uncovering them and warming them with her body heat. This act brought comfort to Boaz, allowing him to sleep soundly.

At midnight, Boaz woke up and turned, surprised to find a woman at his feet. "Who are you?" he asked. Ruth responded, *"I am your servant Ruth. Spread the corner of your garment over me, for you are a guardian-redeemer of our family." Boaz replied, "The Lord bless you, my daughter. This kindness is greater than what you have shown earlier; you did not run after younger men, rich or poor. Don't be afraid, my daughter. I will do for you all you ask. Everyone in town knows you are a woman of noble character. While it is true I am a guardian-redeemer for our family, there is another who is more closely related. Stay here tonight, and in the morning, if he wishes to perform his duty as guardian-redeemer, let him. But if he is unwilling, as surely as the Lord lives, I will fulfill the role. Lie here until morning" (Ruth 3:9-13).*

Boaz, nearly twice Ruth's age, was surprised that she did not choose one of the wealthy young men, which likely explains why he hadn't pursued her initially. Ruth adhered to Boaz's instructions and remained at his feet. When morning arrived, they both rose before anyone else. Boaz then filled Ruth's cloak with six measures of barley, secured it, and placed it on her shoulder to carry. Ruth blessed Boaz with her presence, and he reciprocated by providing for her materially, and emotionally.

The Redeemer's Decision

Back in the city, Naomi waited anxiously for Ruth's return. When Ruth arrived home, Naomi promptly asked her to recount everything that happened that night. Ruth complied and shared all of Boaz's words and actions, also mentioning that he had given her a coat filled with barley. Naomi received it happily and advised Ruth to be patient and to wait and see what would happen next. They were both confident in Boaz's intentions.

Early the next morning, Boaz went to the city's gate and waited for his fellow kinsman to arrive. Upon seeing him, Boaz pulled him aside and indicated he had an important matter to discuss. Boaz was well-prepared, having already assembled ten elders from the city as witnesses. He informed his kinsman that their relative Naomi was selling a piece of land that had belonged to her deceased husband Elimelech. Boaz explained that whoever purchased the land would also need to marry Ruth the Moabitess to continue her deceased husband's lineage.

The kinsman responded to Boaz, stating, "I cannot redeem the land for myself, as doing so would jeopardize my own inheritance. I give you permission to purchase it in my place." To finalize this agreement, an old tradition required a man to take off his shoes and give them to the other party. The kinsman removed his shoes and gave them to Boaz in the presence of the ten elders. Boaz then declared to the elders, "You are witnesses today that I have purchased from Naomi all that belonged to Elimelech and his sons Mahlon and Chilion. This includes Ruth, the wife of Mahlon, whom I have acquired to be my wife to perpetuate the name of her deceased husband."

The elders and all the people at the gate proclaimed, "We are witnesses. May the Lord make the woman entering your house like Rachel and Leah, whose children built the house of Israel. May you achieve fame in Ephrathah and Bethlehem. Let your house be like the house of Pharez, where the Lord blessed Tamar to bear a son; may He do similarly for you and this woman as well" (Ruth 4:11-12). Their statement was both prophetic and affirming, especially since Boaz was advanced in age and Ruth had remained childless from her previous marriage.

From Widow to Matriarch

"So Boaz took Ruth into his home, and she became his wife. When he slept with her, the Lord enabled her to become pregnant, and she gave birth to a son." (Ruth 4:13). It was by God's intervention that Ruth conceived! Despite not being able to have children during her ten years in Moab, Ruth became pregnant on her wedding night in Bethlehem, the land flowing with milk and honey. Her faith in God restored her! Ruth gave birth to a son named Obed. The unexpected happened, and Ruth was now a mother!

Naomi witnessed the blessing of Obed's birth. She knew Ruth's story, as did the women of the city. They said to Naomi, "Blessed be the Lord who has not left you without family because this baby will be famous throughout Israel! This child will restore your hope and give you strength in your old age. Your daughter-in-law, who loves you so much, is better to you than seven sons." (Ruth 4:14-15).

God blessed Naomi through Ruth, and Ruth graciously allowed Naomi to care for the child. "And the women her neighbors gave him a name, saying, 'A son has been born to Naomi,' and they called him Obed. He was the father of Jesse, the father of David" (Ruth 4:17).

Ruth's choice to follow Naomi was a pivotal decision that led her to this destiny. Boaz married Ruth and through divine intervention, she bore a son named Obed. This son became a blessing not only to Ruth but also to Naomi, who cared for him. Obed, in turn, was the grandfather of King David, placing Ruth in the lineage that would ultimately lead to Jesus Christ. This story highlights God's providence and the transformative power of faith and loyalty, showcasing Ruth's journey from a childless widow to a revered matriarch in biblical history.

From faith to FEBA (Faith, Endurance, Blessings, and Abundance), Ruth's life is a testament to the power of unwavering belief and the rewards it brings. Her story inspires generations to trust in divine providence and to remain steadfast in faith amidst life's challenges.

BUT RUTH REPLIED, ...YOUR PEOPLE WILL BE MY PEOPLE AND YOUR GOD MY GOD. (RUTH 1:16)

Cantrice's Commentary:
Part Two: Ruth, the Unexpected Matriarch

Although I am not Ruth, I can connect to her story. For several years, my mother-in-law resided with my husband and me. As her caregiver, I understood the dynamics between Ruth and Naomi, which evolved from comfort to discomfort and from familiarity to unfamiliarity. This relationship was based on lived experience, fostering trust to overcome challenges and achieve rewards.

The book of Ruth begins with a sad narrative about a young woman who, through no fault of her own, was born and raised in a land that did not allow her to grow. In Moab, a barren land notorious for incest and human sacrifice, Ruth was married but was unable to produce children even after ten years. Tragically, her husband died, taking with him any chance of motherhood.

After the death of her husband Mahlon, Ruth became very close to her mother-in-law Naomi, whose decision to return to her homeland of Judah would forever change her life. Ruth's journey from Moab to Judah was more than just a move; it involved significant spiritual and cultural changes. She left her past behind and assumed a new identity in a foreign land. Her faith and determination in the face of challenges are a powerful reminder of her strength—a story many women can see themselves in when overcoming life's difficulties.

Like Ruth, I relocated to another state at a young age and benefited from the experience. For today's women, Ruth's story offers several valuable insights.

First, it highlights the importance of loyalty and sisterhood among women. Ruth's relationship with Naomi shows that the strong bonds between women can provide the emotional strength needed to navigate trying times. In a world where women often face difficult challenges, fostering supportive relationships can be a key source of strength.

Secondly, Ruth's solid faith and courage are timeless qualities that connect deeply with modern women. Her willingness to embrace change and step into the unknown serves as an inspirational model for those facing personal or professional transitions. Whether it's changing careers, moving to a new city, or starting a new chapter in life, Ruth's story encourages women to trust in their journey and the potential for positive outcomes.

Thirdly, Ruth demonstrated the benefits of steadfast belief, strength, and the pursuit of a higher purpose. Her story underscores the idea that even in the face of great adversity, faith and loyalty can lead to unimaginable blessings. Ruth's journey encourages both men and women to remain hopeful and courageous, embracing their own paths with the same spirit of determination.

In the end, Ruth had the child she always dreamed of. Her firm belief and dedication paid off. She became the daughter in-law of Rathab, the wife of Boaz, the mother of Obed, and the great-grandmother of King David, earning her place in the history of important biblical figures. Her life story continues to inspire generations of women to trust in divine guidance and stay strong in their faith, no matter what life throws at them. Her story, which started with so much sadness, ended with blessings and abundance!

Cantrice

Summary of Ruth:
Key Points and Scriptures

Introduction

The story of Ruth is a captivating narrative of loyalty, faith, and divine providence set during the era of the judges in Israel. Ruth's journey from a childless widow in Moab to a revered matriarch in Israel underscores the transformative power of unwavering faith and loyalty.

Key Points

- Ruth's Background: Ruth was a Moabite woman who married Mahlon, an Israelite, but remained childless for ten years. After the deaths of her husband and father-in-law, Ruth formed a deep bond with her mother-in-law, Naomi (Ruth 1:1-5).
- Loyalty to Naomi: Despite Naomi's urging to return to her family, Ruth chose to stay with Naomi, declaring, "Your people will be my people and your God my God" (Ruth 1:16-17).
- Journey to Bethlehem: Ruth and Naomi traveled from Moab to Bethlehem, where Ruth began gleaning in the fields of Boaz, a relative of Naomi's late husband (Ruth 1:19-22).
- Meeting Boaz: Ruth's diligence and loyalty impressed Boaz, who blessed her and ensured her safety and provision. Boaz praised Ruth's kindness and courage (Ruth 2:11-12).
- Boaz as Guardian-Redeemer: Boaz took on the role of guardian-redeemer, marrying Ruth to preserve her deceased husband's lineage. Through this union, Ruth bore a son named Obed (Ruth 4:13-17).

Scriptures

Ruth 1:16-17: *"But Ruth replied, 'Don't urge me to leave you or to turn back from you. Where you go I will go, and where you stay I will stay. Your people will be my people and your God my God. Where you die I will die, and there I will be buried. May the Lord deal with me, be it ever so severely, if even death separates you and me.'"*

Ruth 2:11-12: *"Boaz replied, 'I've been told all about what you have done for your mother-in-law since the death of your husband— how you left your father and mother and your homeland and came to live with a people you did not know before. May the Lord repay you for what you have done. May you be richly rewarded by the Lord, the God of Israel, under whose wings you have come to take refuge.'"*

Ruth 4:13-17: *"So Boaz took Ruth and she became his wife. When he made love to her, the Lord enabled her to conceive, and she gave birth to a son. The women said to Naomi: 'Praise be to the Lord, who this day has not left you without a guardian-redeemer. May he become famous throughout Israel! He will renew your life and sustain you in your old age. For your daughter-in-law, who loves you and who is better to you than seven sons, has given him birth.'"*

Conclusion

Ruth's story is a powerful testament to the impact of faith, loyalty, and divine providence. Her journey from a foreign widow to the great-grandmother of King David highlights God's redemptive power and the importance of steadfast belief. Ruth's narrative continues to inspire generations, demonstrating how unwavering faith can lead to unimaginable blessings and a legacy that transcends time.

The Woman at the Well
The Unexpected Evangelist

The woman at the well is the least known of the three women featured in this book. Unlike Rahab and Ruth, who are mentioned by name, she is identified solely by her nationality and the site of her encounter with Jesus Christ. Despite her anonymity, her story might be considered the most remarkable because of her direct meeting with the Savior. It is with this perspective that I share her narrative.

To start, the woman at the well was a Samaritan. Biblically, Samaria refers to the central highland region of ancient Israel, bordered by Galilee to the north and Judea to the south. The term Samaria denotes both a city and an area, meaning "watch mountain." Following their conquest of the Promised Land, the Israelites assigned this region to the tribes of Manasseh and Ephraim, descendants of Joseph. This ancestry attributed Jewish and Hebrew lineage to the woman at the well. Samaria was historically significant and maintained its influence throughout both Old and New Testament times.

During the era of the Judges in the Old Testament, Samaritans faced such severe oppression that they cried out to God, who responded by sending an angel to Gideon. Found near Ophrah's oak, threshing wheat in a winepress, Gideon later led an army, reduced by God's command from 32,000 to 300 men to a miraculous victory over Midianite and Amalekite forces on Mount Gilboa in northern Samaria. Gideon's legacy extended into the New Testament, positioning him as a hero of faith. Gideon, a Samaritan from Manasseh, shares his lineage with the woman at the well.

Jesus and Samaria

The animosity between the Jews and Samaritans persisted well into the first century. Many devout Jews would go out of their way to avoid passing through Samaria. However, Jesus did not follow this custom; he had a unique relationship with Samaria, actively engaging with them and connecting others to their story. In Luke 10:25-37, Jesus narrates the parable of the "good Samaritan," where two significant Jewish figures, a priest and a Levite, failed to assist a wounded stranger. Instead, a Samaritan helped the stranger, took him to an inn, and covered his expenses. Jesus made it clear that the "good Samaritan" is the one who shows love and mercy to his neighbor.

Jesus' second major interaction with Samaritans occurred when on his way from Judea to Galilee, he chose not to bypass Samaria, leading to his encounter with the woman at the well. This event was notable for several reasons: it broke Jewish customs as Jewish men did not converse with Samaritan women, it happened despite ongoing tensions between Jews and Samaritans, and remarkably, Jesus revealed himself as the Messiah to her. This revelation was astonishing because it seemed unlikely that a Samaritan woman would be deemed worthy of such an encounter.

A deeper look into biblical texts shows that the woman at the well's connection with the Messiah began long before their meeting. When Jesus traveled through Samaria, he and his disciples reached Sychar, identified in the Old Testament as Shechem, home to Jacob's well. Sychar, a significant place linked to Jacob and Joseph, provided the woman at the well with historical access to the Messiah. Although

Jesus did not disclose to his disciples "why" he needed to go through Samaria, its ties to Jewish ancestry likely played a role. Jesus, spiritually aware that someone in Samaria needed him, went to Jacob's well. Tired, he sat by the well around noon, sending his disciples to buy food. Soon after, a Samaritan woman came to draw water.

The encounter was notable because the woman chose to draw water at midday rather than in the morning, possibly to avoid others. At Jacob's well, she encountered Jesus by himself. Given the strained relations between Jews and Samaritans, she did not anticipate him initiating a conversation. Nevertheless, Jesus unexpectedly asked her for a drink, a rare interaction as Jews generally did not communicate with Samaritans. She said to him, "You are a Jew, and I am a Samaritan woman. How can you ask me for a drink when the Jews do not associate with Samaritans?

In John 4:10, Jesus responded to her surprise by saying, "If you knew the gift of God and who it is that asks you for a drink, you would have asked him, and he would have given you living water." The woman, both shocked and intrigued, recognized something special about Jesus. She noticed he had nothing to draw water with and questioned the concept of living water, comparing it to the water from Jacob's well. Jesus explained that ordinary water would only provide temporary relief, while the living water he offered would satisfy spiritual thirst permanently.

The idea of never having to draw water again appealed to the woman, considering the effort involved in carrying water daily. Fascinated by Jesus' promise of water leading to eternal life, she requested, "Give me this water to drink so that I will never thirst or come here to draw water again" (John 4:15).

Facing her Truth at the Well

Amazingly, the woman at the well was face-to-face with the savior of the world, and without any physical proof, she chose to believe him at his word. Her request to Jesus to give her drink was more than a mere request for water, it was an affirmation of faith! And this faith was going to be the catalyst for her change. Although Jesus would require more of her that just her statement of faith, like the woman with the issue of blood in Luke chapter eight, it would be her faith that would make her whole.

Unfortunately, she could not achieve completeness without confronting the issues that constrained her. Her fractured relationships significantly limited her life. Addressing this crucial problem would be a pivotal moment for her. Like many, dealing with personal challenges can feel intimidating and overwhelming. The woman at the well must have anxiously awaited Jesus' response. Then it occurred— Jesus addressed her issue directly and urged her to confront the fragmented aspects of her life. "Jesus said to her, go, call your husband, and come here" (John 4:16 ESV).

What options did she have? Deep down, she knew she wasn't married. In today's vernacular, her relationship would have labeled as "complicated," and she didn't want to delve into specifics right then. This would be the pivotal moment in her life! She could either keep hiding or confront the reality. Rather than fabricate a story, she revealed the truth to Jesus and replied candidly, "I don't have a husband."

Jesus did not ask with the intention of embarrassing her. He was already aware of her relationship status but asked to start a conversation about her complicated situation. "Jesus said to her, you are right in saying, I have no husband, for you have had five husbands, and the one that you have now is not your husband. What you have said is true" (John 4:17,18 ESV). Jesus addressed the issue directly because the woman's relationships with men were intricate and complex.

When she mentioned she did not have a husband, Jesus confirmed that she was being honest. Interestingly, Jesus did not imply that she had been married to five different men, as the fifth would still be considered her husband if they were currently married. it's also worth noting that Jesus did not imply the man she was with belonged to another woman; he simply stated that he was not her husband. Importantly, the Bible does not describe her as an adulterer. So, what was her relationship status? For her and women in similar situations, it remained "complicated."

The Defining Instant of Genuine Truth

Jesus then disclosed a significant reality to her: she had been involved with six men, none of whom were her husband. These men were open to sharing intimacy with her but opted not to marry her. The woman at the well found herself perpetually in the role of a girlfriend, never ascending to that of a wife. Having experienced multiple intimate relationships without the commitment of marriage, she was burdened with such shame that she resorted to drawing water at noon to avoid others. This avoidance merely postponed addressing the issues. It is only through confronting our challenges that we can find resolution.

When Jesus instructed her to call her husband, she changed the topic, saying: "I understand that you are a prophet, so explain why our ancestors worshiped on this mountain, but you Jews assert the correct place of worship is in Jerusalem." Even though Jesus recognized that she was changing the subject, he still responded to her question, saying, "Woman, believe me, the time is coming when you will worship the Father neither on this mountain nor in Jerusalem. You Samaritans worship what you do not know; we worship what we do know, for salvation comes from the Jews. However, the time is approaching and is now here when true worshipers will worship the Father in spirit and in truth, for these are the kinds of worshipers the Father seeks. God is spirit, and his worshipers must worship in spirit and in truth" (John 4:21-24 NIV). In doing so, Jesus shifted the conversation towards her relationship with God rather than focusing on her relationships with men.

Jesus created a safe environment for her to express her vulnerability by steering the conversation toward her relationship with God. Although she was a Samarian, she had heard about the Messiah, known as the Christ, who would teach and explain everything. Could this be him? Jesus then affirmed her belief by stating, "I, the one speaking to you—I am he" (John 4:26). It was a moment of significant faith and transformation! She confronted her brokenness in front of him, revealing her scars, and instead of shaming her, Jesus disclosed his identity to her. By addressing her reality, this Samaritan woman, shunned by her society, was graced to be in the presence of the Messiah!

Apart from his disciples, Jesus had never disclosed he was the Messiah to anyone. What was special about this Samaritan woman that prompted him to do so? Was it her honesty about her broken life, or her bold declaration that she sought the Messiah who would explain everything? We may not know for certain, but we do know that this foreign woman with a complicated past met Jesus and engaged in an open, honest conversation. Her vulnerability moved Jesus to reveal himself to her.

What about contemporary women in similar circumstances? How might they respond to public scrutiny? Would they conceal their vulnerabilities or face them head-on and triumph? The Samaritan woman made her decision, and despite being initially rejected by many, she was ultimately accepted by the King of Kings and the Lord of Lords. Her conversation transformed her life. Much like Rahab's story where the Bible declared that Joshua saved Rahab, Jesus saved the woman at the well. Salvation reached her heart, bringing her such immense joy that she abandoned her waterpots and hurried back into town to spread the news.

The Unlikely Evangelist

As she rushed to Samaria, she thought about her meeting with the Messiah. He was aware of her past without judging her. He recognized her fatigue and offered her refreshing water, saw her shattered life and provided eternal life. This experience turned into a profound testimony for her and others in similar situations, showing that those rejected by society are accepted by God. Like Rahab and Ruth, the woman at the well exemplifies the transformative power of faith.

When the disciples returned, they were surprised to see Jesus talking with a Samaritan woman. Although puzzled, they did not press for answers. This moment marked the beginning of Jews interacting with Samaritans. Noticing that Jesus hadn't eaten, the disciples offered him food, but he declined, saying that helping the woman nourished him and fulfilling God's will was his sustenance. Misunderstanding, the disciples thought someone else had fed him, so Jesus clarified that his true nourishment came from doing God's work.

The Samaritan woman hurried back to her town to tell the men, "Come see a man who told me everything I ever did! Could this be the Messiah?" Her newfound enthusiasm persuaded many townspeople to go with her to meet Jesus. Surprisingly, these men, who once shunned her, now followed her lead. They listened to Jesus at the well and believed. As noted in John 4:39-42, "Many of the Samaritans from that town believed in him because of the woman's testimony, 'He told me everything I ever did.' When the Samaritans came to him, they urged him to stay with them, and he stayed two days. Because of his words, many more became believers. They said to the woman, 'We no longer believe just because of what you said; now we have heard for ourselves, and we know that this man really is the Savior of the world.'"

"BUT YOU WILL RECEIVE POWER WHEN THE HOLY SPIRIT COMES ON YOU; AND YOU WILL BE MY WITNESSES IN JERUSALEM, AND IN ALL JUDEA AND SAMARIA, AND TO THE ENDS OF THE EARTH." (ACTS 1:8, NIV)

John 4:39 notes that many Samaritans believed in Jesus because of the woman's testimony. At the well, she became an evangelist, guiding others to Christ. Her past wasn't a hindrance but a part of her story. God uses broken individuals for amazing purposes! Jesus turned her struggles into victories and her challenges into a testimony. This transformation is possible for anyone brave enough to be sincere with God.

The Timeless Relevance of the Woman at the Well

First, the story of the woman at the well transcends its historical roots, offering a timeless message that continues to resonate with women today. Her transformation from shame and marginalization to acceptance and purpose reflects the struggles and triumphs experienced by many women across various times and cultures. Just as the Samaritan woman faced societal judgment and personal difficulties, contemporary women often are confronted with challenges that test their faith and perseverance. Her encounter at Jacob's well serves as a touching reminder that regardless of how isolated or unworthy one may feel, there is always a possibility for redemption and renewal.

Secondly, the woman at the well's honest reflection on her past and transformative dialogue with Jesus inspire modern women to embrace their vulnerabilities. Her journey from outcast to evangelist highlights the empowering potential of faith, encouraging openness and the courage to seek help and healing. Women today can find strength in her story, showing how faith can turn perceived weaknesses into powerful strengths.

Thirdly, the woman at the well's immediate response to share her experience with her community reflects the ripple effect of personal transformation. Like her, women today have the power to influence and inspire those around them. Her story is a testament to the enduring impact one can have when they are willing to step forward and share their truth.

Finally, the woman at the well leaves a legacy of hope and redemption. Her story is a beacon for modern women, illuminating the possibilities that lie beyond their current struggles. It affirms that every woman, regardless of her past, has the potential to write a new narrative filled with purpose, dignity, and grace.

From faith to FEBA (Faith, Endurance, Blessings, and Abundance), the story of the woman at the well teaches valuable lessons. By adopting her perspective, modern women are reminded that their value isn't determined by their past but by their faith and the transformative power of divine love. The woman at the well's narrative remains an inspiration, urging women to trust in their journey and in the endless opportunities that faith can bring.

Cantrice's Commentary:
Part Three: The Woman at the Well –
The Unexpected Evangelist

I can relate with the story of the woman at the well. Developing a relationship with Christ provides a distinct perspective on awareness. I am now able to reflect and forgive myself because Jesus forgave me. I had to be honest in my truth because I was lost. Thank God for Jesus! Like me, many individuals can relate to the unnamed woman at the well. Her encounter is a perfect example of grace and mercy.

The woman at the well, being in the moment of an uncomfortable conversation, chose not to leave. When Jesus said, "Go get your husband," knowing that she did not have one, let her know that he knew her story. It's comforting to know that Jesus sees our flaws and still believes in our potential.

The Samaritan woman had an open and honest exchange with him, who asked her for a drink of water. This straightforward conversation allowed her to share her flaws and imperfections without feeling judged. Feeling forgiven helped her forgive herself, and become more self-aware, transforming her life. The deep conversation with the Messiah, who knew everything about her, healed her brokenness, and restored every area of lack in her life.

John 4:14 states, "But whoever drinks of the water that I will give him will never be thirsty again." The water that I will give him will become in him a spring of water welling up to eternal life." The woman at the well was able to share this experience with others, who then established their own relationship with the Savior.

A relation indicates a connection, while a relationship explains its nature and depth. The story of the woman at the well shows how deepening a bond with Christ can lead to personal transformation. This transformation highlights Jesus' power and love, showing that a meaningful connection with him can change lives in extraordinary ways.

Just as the Samaritan woman experienced profound change through her encounter with Jesus, we are invited to seek and deepen our own relationships with him. By modeling her actions—approaching Jesus openly, and with a desire for truth—we too can experience transformative growth and a closer connection with God.

Cantrice

Summary of The Woman at the Well

Introduction

The story of the Samaritan woman at the well, found in John 4:1-42, is a powerful testament to transformation and redemption. Her encounter with Christ at Jacob's well not only changed her life but also impacted her entire community.

Key Points

- Divine Appointment: Jesus intentionally travels through Samaria and initiates a conversation with a Samaritan woman, breaking cultural norms (John 4:4-9).
- Living Water: Jesus offers her "living water," symbolizing eternal life and spiritual fulfillment (John 4:10-14).
- Revelation of Truth: Jesus reveals His knowledge of her past and present, demonstrating His divine insight (John 4:16-18).
- Declaration of the Messiah: Jesus openly declares Himself as the Messiah to her, a rare revelation in His ministry (John 4:25-26).
- Witness and Transformation: The woman, transformed by the encounter, leaves her water jar and shares her experience with her community, leading many to believe in Jesus (John 4:28-30, 39-42).

Scriptures

- John 4:4-9 – Jesus travels through Samaria and speaks to the Samaritan woman.
- John 4:10-14 – Jesus offers the living water.
- John 4:16-18 – Jesus reveals His knowledge of her life.
- John 4:25-26 – Jesus declares Himself as the Messiah.
- John 4:28-30, 39-42 – The woman's testimony leads many to faith.

Conclusion

The Samaritan woman's immediate response to share her experience with her community reflects the powerful effect of personal transformation. Her story is a beacon of hope and redemption, demonstrating that one's past does not define their future. This narrative encourages modern women to embrace their faith and trust in the transformative power of divine love. Just as the woman at the well left a legacy of hope, each woman today holds the potential to inspire and influence those around them, stepping forward to share their truth and experience God's transformative power in their lives.

The Transformative
Impact of God on Women's Lives

In Summary, women have always been integral to God's plan for humanity. Eve, the first woman and mother of all living beings, set the precedent. Sarai, whose name was later changed to Sarah meaning "woman of nobility," was pivotal as the first lady of the promise God made to Abraham. She, along with Rahab, is celebrated as a hero of faith in Hebrews chapter 11. Named or unnamed, women throughout history have believed in God's power for miraculous outcomes. "Women received their dead raised to life again: and others were tortured, not accepting deliverance; that they might obtain a better resurrection" (Hebrews 11:35). The Bible chronicles many women who trusted God for greater things, confronting moments of faith and emerging victorious.

The stories of Rahab, Ruth, and the Samaritan woman at the well serve as powerful narratives of faith, transformation, and divine redemption. These women, though coming from different backgrounds, all experienced profound changes in their lives through their encounters with God. Rahab's story exemplifies that no past is too tainted for redemption and that faith can pave the way for a legacy of honor and grace. Ruth's narrative highlights the blessings that come with steadfast faithfulness and the transformative power of divine providence. The Samaritan woman at the well's story is a beacon of hope and redemption, demonstrating that one's past does not define their future.

These stories collectively teach that faith, courage, and loyalty can lead to transformation and restoration. Each woman, through her unique journey, illustrates that God's grace is available to all, regardless of their past or present circumstances. As we reflect on their legacies, we are reminded of the potential within each of us to inspire and influence those around us, stepping forward to share our truths and experience God's transformative power in our lives.

Now, at your FEBA (Faith, Endurance, Blessings, and Abundance) moment, what will you do? Will you face this turning point and press forward beyond it? Like the unnamed women hailed as heroes of faith, will you continue to believe steadfastly, assured of receiving God's best in the resurrection? Within you lies the power to choose. When you decide to move past FEBA and delve deeper into faith, you will encounter God's transformative power in your life. From faith to FEBA, the prostitute, the widow, and the woman at the well. God's transformational power in the lives of women!

ABOUT THE AUTHORS

Tim Houston and Cantrice Houston are passionate about helping others improve their relationship with God. As a blended family with 8 children and 18 grandchildren, they understand the importance of faith, family, and community. Their journey together has been marked by a deep commitment to spiritual growth and a desire to inspire others through their experiences.

Tim brings a wealth of knowledge and leadership to their shared mission. His dedication to faith and family is evident in every aspect of his life. Cantrice, with her nurturing spirit and unwavering faith, complements Tim's vision, creating a powerful partnership that resonates with readers.

Together, they have authored "From Faith to FEBA: The Prostitute, the Widow, and the Woman at the Well; God's Transformational Power in the Lives of Women," a book that celebrates the inclusion and triumph of women who, despite their circumstances, chose faith over fear and witnessed God's transformative power. Through their writing, Tim and Cantrice aim to encourage readers to recognize and embrace their own "Faith to FEBA" moments, leading to profound personal transformation and a deeper relationship with God.

From Faith to FEBA

The Prostitute, the Widow, and the Woman at the Well

Moving toward your FEBA
Faith, Endurance, Blessing, and Abundance

www.ingramcontent.com/pod-product-compliance
Lightning Source LLC
Chambersburg PA
CBHW031226090426

42740CB00007B/723